Easy Chicago Cookbook

Authentic Chicago Recipes from the Windy City for Delicious Chicago Cooking

By
BookSumo Press

Published by
http://www.booksumo.com

LEGAL NOTES

Table of Contents

Chicago Cod Chowder 6

Windy City Vegetarian Chili 7

Windy City Duck Roasted 8

Chicago Style Italian Dip 9

Chicago Winter Stew 10

Sunday Breakfast Bread 11

Creamy Chicken and Rice Soup with Fresh Italian Herbs 12

Chicago Style Brownies 13

Faggioli Soup 14

Latin Big Star Green Salsa from Chicago 15

Skirt Steak Chicago Style 17

Greek 5-Ingredient Soup 18

Little Chicago Sliders 19

Randolph Street Risotto 20

Chicago Dough for Deep Dish Homemade Pizzas 21

Buffalo Grove Inspired Salad Dressing 22

Illinois Potato Burritos 23

Italian Beef Lunch Box 25

Chicago Mercantile Inspired Cocktail 26

Sloppy Joes Windy City Style 27

Chicago Corn Casserole 28

Chicago Monday Minestrone 29

5-Ingredient Chicago Penne Pesto 30

Chicago Hot Dog Salad 31

Chicago Mac and Cheese 32

Downtown Chicago Egg Salad 33

Hot to Make Chicago Pizza Dough 34

Rogers Park Inspired Risotto 35

Cook County Vegetable Mash 36

Authentic Chicago Style Shrimp 37

How to Make Chicago Style Pizza Sauce 38

Chicago Haddock Chowder 39

Chicago Chicken Cutlet 40

Relish for Hot Dogs Chicago Style 41

Fried Chicken with White Sauce 42

Chicago Deep Dish At-Home 43

Windy City Chicago Hot Dogs 44

Italian Beef Chicago Style 45

Blackhawks Inspired Party Dip 46

Chicago Country Winter Soup 47

Chicago Buttermilk Pizza Bites 48

Chicago Public School Pilaf 49

Back-to-School Cookies 50

Lincolnshire Balsamic Soup 51

Chi-Town Cake 52

Downers Grove Steak Rolls 53

Alternative Chicago Hot Dogs 54

Authentic Italian Antipasto 55

Classical Alfredo 56

Easy Italian Parmigiana 57

Classical Spanish Beef Patties 58

Pastelon 59

Bistec Encebollao 60

Alternative Windy City Chicken and Rice Soup 61

Tostones 62

Steaks in Chicago 63

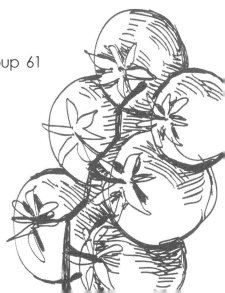

CHICAGO
Cod Chowder

Prep Time: 15 mins
Total Time: 1 hr

Servings per Recipe: 8
Calories   379 kcal
Fat   15.5 g
Carbohydrates   30.7g
Protein   28.7 g
Cholesterol   80 mg
Sodium   612 mg

Ingredients

1 lb. sliced turkey bacon
1 large onion, chopped
5 medium potatoes, peeled and diced
1 1/2 lb. cod fillets, cut into 1 inch
cubes
1 (12 fluid oz.) can evaporated milk

1/2 C. whole milk
2 tbsp butter
salt and pepper to taste

Directions

1. Heat a large pan on medium-high heat and cook the bacon till browned completely.
2. Transfer the bacon onto a paper towel lined plate to drain and then crumble it.
3. Drain the grease, reserving about 1 tbsp in the pan.
4. Place the pan on medium and sauté the onions for about 5 minutes.
5. Add the potatoes and enough water to cover them and bring to a boil.
6. Cook for about 5 minutes.
7. Stir in the fish pieces, evaporated milk, whole milk and butter and bring to a boil.
8. Reduce the heat to low heat and simmer for about 30 minutes.
9. Stir in the salt and pepper and remove from the heat.
10. Serve hot with a topping of the crumbled bacon.

Windy City
Vegetarian Chili

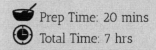

Prep Time: 20 mins
Total Time: 7 hrs

Servings per Recipe: 12
Calories	160 kcal
Fat	4.7 g
Carbohydrates	24.8g
Protein	7.1 g
Cholesterol	0 mg
Sodium	409 mg

Ingredients

2 cubes vegetable bouillon, crumbled
1 tbsp ground cumin
1 clove garlic, minced
2 tsp chili powder
1 tsp ground turmeric
1 tsp dried oregano
1 tsp dried basil
1 tsp ground red pepper
1 C. water
1 (15 oz.) can black beans, rinsed and drained
1 (15 oz.) can dark red kidney beans,

drained and rinsed
1 (15 oz.) can vegetarian baked beans
1 (14.5 oz.) can diced tomatoes
1 onion, diced
2 stalks celery, diced
1 C. diced carrot
1 C. fresh green beans, trimmed and cut into
3/4-inch pieces
1 C. coconut milk

Directions

1. In a small pan, mix together the vegetable bouillon, cumin, garlic, chili powder, turmeric, oregano, basil and red pepper on low heat and cook for about 1-2 minutes.
2. Add the water and bring to a simmer.
3. Remove from the heat.
4. In a slow cooker, mix together the black beans, red kidney beans, vegetarian baked beans, tomatoes, onion, celery, carrot, green beans and spice mixture.
5. Set the slow cooker on High and cook, covered for about 6-8 hours.
6. Stir in the coconut milk.
7. Now, set the slow cooker on Low and cook, covered for about 30 minutes.

WINDY CITY
Duck Roasted

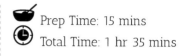

Prep Time: 15 mins
Total Time: 1 hr 35 mins

Servings per Recipe: 4

Calories	389 kcal
Fat	31.3 g
Carbohydrates	4.5g
Protein	21.8 g
Cholesterol	91 mg
Sodium	163 mg

Ingredients

1 (4 lb.) whole duck
1 tbsp garlic powder
1 tbsp onion powder

salt and pepper, to taste
2 tbsp caraway seeds

Directions

1. Set your oven to 425 degrees F before doing anything else. And arrange a rack in a roasting pan.
2. Wash the duck and with the paper towels, pat dry.
3. With a sharp knife, score the breast and legs by cutting into skin going 2/3 of the way through the skin, being careful not to slice into meat.
4. Rub the cavity and the outside of the duck with the garlic powder, onion powder, salt and pepper evenly.
5. Sprinkle the caraway seeds over the duck and into scored skin.
6. Arrange the duck over the rack in the roasting pan, breast side up.
7. Cook in the oven for about 15 minutes.
8. Now, place the duck, breast side down and cook in the oven for about 15 minutes.
9. Remove the duck from the oven and set your oven to 350 degrees F.
10. Now, place the duck, breast side up and cook in the oven for about 20 minutes.
11. Now, place the duck, breast side down and cook in the oven for about 20 minutes.
12. Remove duck from oven and keep aside for about 10 minutes before serving.

Chicago Style
Italian Dip

Prep Time: 5 mins
Total Time: 25 mins

Servings per Recipe: 32
Calories	49 kcal
Fat	3 g
Carbohydrates	1.5g
Protein	3.7 g
Cholesterol	16 mg
Sodium	165 mg

Ingredients

1 (1.37 oz.) package McCormick(R) Thick &
Zesty Spaghetti Sauce Mix
1 C. part-skim ricotta cheese
1 egg
2 C. shredded mozzarella cheese, divided

1/2 C. grated Parmesan cheese
1/4 C. mini pepperoni slices

Directions

1. Set your oven to 375 degrees F before doing anything else and grease a 9-inch round cake pan.
2. Prepare the sauce according to package's directions.
3. Remove from the heat and keep aside to cool slightly.
4. In a large bowl, mix together the ricotta cheese, egg, 1 C. of the mozzarella cheese and Parmesan cheese.
5. Place the mixture in the prepared cake pan evenly and top with the prepared spaghetti sauce.
6. Sprinkle with the remaining 1 C. of the mozzarella cheese and pepperoni.
7. Cook in the oven for about 20 minutes or until heated through.

CHICAGO
Winter Stew

Prep Time: 10 mins
Total Time: 10 hrs 10 mins

Servings per Recipe: 6
Calories	668 kcal
Fat	30.5 g
Carbohydrates	61.3g
Protein	36.4 g
Cholesterol	101 mg
Sodium	1128 mg

Ingredients

1 1/2 lbs cubed beef stew meat
1/2 lb smoked sausage of your choice, sliced
1 medium onion, diced

3 potatoes, scrubbed and cubed
1 (28 oz.) can baked beans

Directions

1. Add the following to the crock of a slow cooker: potatoes, stew, onions, and sausage. Stir the mix then top everything with the beans.
2. Place a lid on the crock and cook the stew for 7 hrs with low heat.
3. Enjoy.

Sunday Breakfast Bread

Prep Time: 15 mins
Total Time: 1 hr 25 mins

Servings per Recipe: 12
Calories	264 kcal
Fat	8.9 g
Carbohydrates	43.6 g
Protein	3.8 g
Cholesterol	51 mg
Sodium	223 mg

Ingredients

2 C. all-purpose flour
1 tsp baking soda
1 tsp ground cinnamon
1/4 tsp ground nutmeg
1/4 tsp ground ginger
1/4 tsp salt
1/2 C. butter, softened
1/2 C. white sugar

1/2 C. brown sugar
2 1/3 C. mashed overripe bananas
2 eggs, beaten
1 tbsp lemon juice
1 tsp vanilla extract

Directions

1. Set your oven to 350 degrees F before doing anything else and lightly, grease a 9x5-inch loaf pan.
2. In a bowl, mix together the flour, baking soda, cinnamon, nutmeg, ginger and salt.
3. In another bowl, add the butter, white sugar and brown sugar and with an electric mixer, beat till smooth and creamy.
4. Add the bananas, eggs, lemon juice, and vanilla extract and mix till well combined.
5. Add the banana mixture into the flour mixture and mix till just combined.
6. Place the mix into the prepared loaf pan evenly.
7. Cook in the oven for about 60-65 minutes or till a toothpick inserted in the center comes out clean.
8. Remove from the oven and keep onto the wire rack to cool in the pan for about 10 minutes.
9. Carefully, invert the bread onto the wire rack to cool completely.

CREAMY CHICKEN
and Rice Soup with Fresh Italian Herbs

 Prep Time: 15 mins
Total Time: 1 hr

Servings per Recipe: 12
Calories   137 kcal
Fat   5.5 g
Carbohydrates   13.6 g
Protein   8.2 g
Cholesterol   20 mg
Sodium   274 mg

Ingredients

2 tbsps olive oil
2 skinless, boneless chicken breast
halves - shredded
salt and pepper to taste
1 tbsp butter
1/2 small onion, chopped
2 cloves garlic, finely chopped
3 tbsps all-purpose flour
10 sprigs Italian flat leaf parsley

3 sprigs fresh thyme
1 bay leaf
3 C. chicken stock
3 C. milk
1 C. water
1 C. uncooked instant rice
1 tsp Cajun spice, optional

Directions

1. Make an herb bundle with some kitchen string: take your thyme, parsley, and bay leaf and tie everything together then place the bundle to the side.
2. Get your olive oil hot in a saucepan then once the oil is hot add in your chicken, pepper, and salt. Let everything cook for 7 mins or until the chicken is done.
3. Place the chicken to the side. Now lower the heat then add in your butter. Let the butter melt then begin to stir fry your garlic and onion in the butter for 6 mins.
4. Add in the flour and stir everything until the flour begins to brown a little.
5. Add your milk and stock to the mix then add in the tied herbs and the chicken as well.
6. Stir everything and let it simmer for 30 mins.
7. Now a get some water boiling in a 2nd pot for your rice. Once the water is boiling combine in your rice, place a lid on the pot, and let everything cook for 7 mins, with a low level of heat.
8. Take out the tied herbs from the pot then add in your rice and your Cajun spice and stir everything again.
9. Enjoy.

Chicago Style Brownies

Prep Time: 15 mins
Total Time: 1 hr

Servings per Recipe: 16

Calories	228 kcal
Fat	9.6 g
Carbohydrates	35.7g
Protein	2.6 g
Cholesterol	23 mg
Sodium	191 mg

Ingredients

2/3 C. gluten-free baking mix (such as Bob's Red Mill All Purpose GF Baking Flour(R))
1/2 C. cornstarch
1 C. white sugar
1 C. packed brown sugar

3/4 C. unsweetened cocoa powder
1 tsp baking soda
2 eggs, beaten
3/4 C. margarine, melted

Directions

1. Set your oven to 350 degrees F before doing anything else and grease an 8x8-inch square baking dish.
2. In a bowl, sift together the baking mix, cornstarch, white sugar, brown sugar, cocoa powder and baking soda.
3. Add the eggs and melted margarine and with an electric mixer, beat on low for about 3-5 minutes.
4. Transfer the mixture into the prepared baking dish evenly.
5. Arrange a piece of foil over the oven rack.
6. Cook in the oven for about 40-45 minutes.

FAGGIOLI
Soup

 Prep Time: 1 hr
Total Time: 3 hrs

Servings per Recipe: 20
Calories	322 kcal
Fat	14.9 g
Carbohydrates	27.1g
Protein	20.6 g
Cholesterol	45 mg
Sodium	783 mg

Ingredients

3 lb. lean ground beef
1/2 C. olive oil
4 C. chopped onion
2 C. chopped celery
2 (4.5 oz.) jars bottled minced garlic
1 tsp coarsely ground black pepper
8 (14 oz.) cans beef broth
1 (28 oz.) can crushed tomatoes
1 (6 oz.) can tomato paste

2 1/2 tsp dried thyme
2 1/2 tsp dried basil
2 1/2 tsp dried oregano
2 tbsp dried parsley
2 C. dintalini pasta
2 (15 oz.) cans kidney beans, drained and rinsed

Directions

1. Heat a large pan on medium heat and cook the beef till browned completely.
2. Drain the excess grease from the skillet and transfer the beef into a bowl.
3. In the same pan, heat the olive oil and cook the onion, celery, garlic and black pepper for about 10 minutes.
4. Stir in the beef broth, crushed tomatoes, tomato paste, thyme, basil, oregano and parsley.
5. Reduce the heat and simmer, covered for about 1 hour.
6. Stir in the beef and simmer for about 15 minutes.
7. Stir in the pasta and cook for about 8-10 minutes.
8. Stir in the beans and cook for about 10-15 minutes.

Latin Big Star
Green Salsa from Chicago

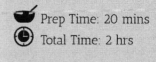

Prep Time: 20 mins

Total Time: 2 hrs

Servings per Recipe: 15
Calories	40 kcal
Fat	3 g
Carbohydrates	3.2g
Protein	0.6 g
Cholesterol	0 mg
Sodium	120 mg

Ingredients

10 fresh tomatillos, husks removed
3 cloves garlic
1 C. water
4 Serrano chilis, stemmed
2 Poblano chilis, stemmed
3 tbsp vegetable oil
1 yellow onion, chopped

1 tsp coarse salt
1/4 C. chopped fresh cilantro
2 tbsp minced red onion
1 tbsp fresh lime juice

Directions

1. In a small pan, add the tomatillos, garlic cloves and water on high heat and bring to a boil.
2. Reduce the heat to medium-low and simmer for about 15-20 minutes.
3. Set the broiler of your oven and arrange oven rack about 6-inch from the heating element.
4. Line a baking sheet with a piece of the foil.
5. Cut the Serrano peppers and Poblano peppers in half from top to bottom and remove the stem, seeds and ribs.
6. Arrange the peppers onto the prepared baking sheet, cut side down.
7. Cook under the broiler for about 3-5 minutes.
8. Transfer the blackened peppers into a bowl and immediately with a plastic wrap, cover tightly.
9. Keep aside to steam for about 5-7 minutes.
10. Remove the blackened skins.
11. Stir the peppers into the simmering tomatillo mixture and cook for about 5 minutes.
12. Remove from the heat and keep aside.

13. In a skillet, heat the vegetable oil on medium heat and cook the yellow onion for about 7-10 minutes.

14. In a blender, add the tomatillo mixture and cooked onion and pulse till smooth.

15. Return the mixture to the skillet on medium-high heat and cook for about 5-7 minutes.

16. Transfer the salsa into a bowl and keep aside in room temperature to cool.

17. After cooling, stir in the salt, cilantro, red onion and lime juice.

18. Serve immediately.

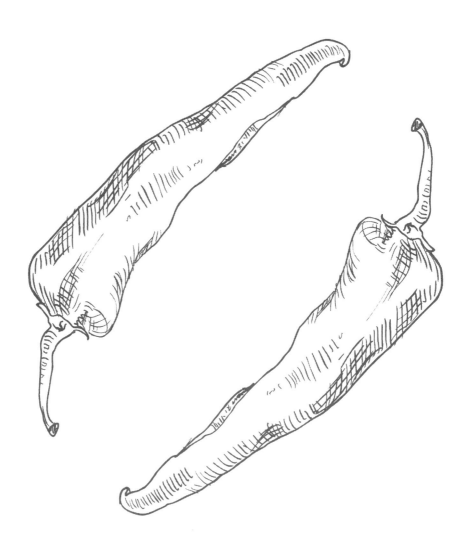

Skirt Steak
Chicago Style

🥣 Prep Time: 20 mins
🕐 Total Time: 8 hrs 45 mins

Servings per Recipe: 16
Calories	404 kcal
Fat	31.7 g
Carbohydrates	12.8g
Protein	14 g
Cholesterol	25 mg
Sodium	491 mg

Ingredients

4 lb. trimmed skirt steaks
2 C. olive oil
1 C. red wine
2 tbsp dried parsley
2 tbsp dried basil
2 tbsp balsamic vinegar

2 tbsp soy sauce
6 cloves garlic, crushed
2 bay leaves
2 C. barbecue sauce

Directions

1. With a sharp knife, make the diagonal cuts through the skirt steak on both sides.
2. Cut diagonally about every 1/4-1/2-inch, then cut diagonally in the opposite, perpendicular direction.
3. Repeat on the other side of the steak.
4. In a large glass bowl, add the olive oil, red wine, parsley, basil, balsamic vinegar, soy sauce, garlic and bay leaves and beat till well combined.
5. Add the skirt steaks and toss to coat well.
6. With a plastic wrap, cover the bowl and refrigerate for at least 8 hours to overnight.
7. Set your outdoor grill for medium heat and lightly, grease the grill grate.
8. Remove the skirt steaks from the bowl and shake off the excess marinade.
9. Discard the remaining marinade.
10. Cook the skirt steak on the grill for about 10 minutes per side.
11. Coat the steaks with the barbecue sauce and cook for about 2 minutes.
12. Flip the steaks and coat with the barbecue sauce and cook for about 2 minutes.

GREEK
5-Ingredient Soup

Prep Time: 20 mins
Total Time: 1 hr

Servings per Recipe: 2
Calories	390 kcal
Fat	12.1 g
Carbohydrates	57.7g
Protein	12.1 g
Cholesterol	24 mg
Sodium	1064 mg

Ingredients

1 (10.75 oz.) can condensed cream of
chicken soup
1 1/4 C. milk
1/2 C. uncooked white rice

1 C. water
2 fluid oz. lemon juice

Directions

1. In a medium pan, mix together the chicken soup and milk and cook till heated completely, beating continuously.
2. In another small pan, add 1 C. of the water and uncooked rice and bring to a boil.
3. Reduce the heat and simmer for about 20 minutes.
4. Transfer the rice into soup and cook till heated completely.
5. Slowly, add the lemon juice and stir to combine.
6. Serve warm.

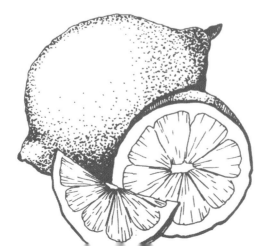

Little Chicago
Sliders

🥣 Prep Time: 15 mins

🕐 Total Time: 25 mins

Servings per Recipe: 24

Calories	155 kcal
Fat	6.2 g
Carbohydrates	16.4g
Protein	8.3 g
Cholesterol	26 mg
Sodium	283 mg

Ingredients

1 1/2 lb. ground chuck
1/3 C. plain bread crumbs
1 egg
1 (1 oz.) package dry onion soup mix
2 tbsp water

1/2 tsp ground black pepper
24 small square dinner rolls

Directions

1. Set your oven to 400 degrees F before doing anything else.
2. In a bowl, add the ground chuck, bread crumbs, egg, onion soup mix, water and black pepper and mix till well combined.
3. Place the mixture into a 10x15-inch jelly roll pan and press to smooth the surface.
4. With a fork, prick the holes through the chuck mixture for ventilation during the cooking.
5. Cook in the oven for about 10 minutes.
6. Remove from the oven and drain the excess grease from the pan.
7. Cut chuck mixture into squares that will fit in the rolls.
8. Place 1 chuck patty in each roll and serve.

RANDOLPH STREET
Risotto

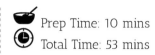

Prep Time: 10 mins
Total Time: 53 mins

Servings per Recipe: 4
Calories	552 kcal
Fat	23 g
Carbohydrates	68.7g
Protein	16.4 g
Cholesterol	48 mg
Sodium	872 mg

Ingredients

3 C. chicken stock
1 bunch spring onions, chopped
5 tbsp butter, divided
1/2 bunch spring garlic, minced
2 C. steel-cut oats
sea salt and freshly ground black
pepper to taste

1/3 C. white wine
1/2 C. grated Parmigiano-Reggiano
cheese

Directions

1. In a small pan, add the chicken stock on medium heat and cook for about 5 minutes.
2. Remove from the heat and keep, aside, covered to keep warm.
3. Reserve 2 tbsp of the spring onion tops.
4. In a large skillet, melt 2 tbsp of the butter on medium heat and sauté the remaining spring onions for about 1 minute.
5. Add the spring garlic and cook for about 2-3 minutes, stirring occasionally.
6. Stir in the oats and cook for about 30 seconds.
7. Stir in 2 tbsp of the butter and cook for about 2 minutes.
8. Stir in the salt, pepper and wine and cook for about 3 minutes.
9. Add enough chicken stock that covers the oats and cook for about 3 minutes, stirring occasionally.
10. Repeat with the remaining stock and cook for about 24 minutes, stirring occasionally.
11. Stir in the reserved spring onion tops and cook for about 1 minute.
12. Reduce the heat to low and stir in the remaining 1 tbsp of the butter and Parmigiano-Reggiano cheese.
13. Cook for about 1 minute. Stir in the salt and pepper and serve.

Chicago Dough
for Deep Dish Homemade Pizzas

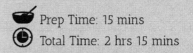

Prep Time: 15 mins
Total Time: 2 hrs 15 mins

Servings per Recipe: 8
Calories	390 kcal
Fat	17.8 g
Carbohydrates	50.9g
Protein	6.4 g
Cholesterol	0 mg
Sodium	584 mg

Ingredients

1 (.25 oz.) package active dry yeast
1/3 C. white sugar
2/3 C. water
2 C. all-purpose flour
1 C. bread flour
1/4 C. corn oil

2 tsp salt
6 tbsp vegetable oil
1/2 C. all-purpose flour

Directions

1. In a bowl, dissolve the yeast and sugar in the water and keep aside for about 5 minutes.
2. In another a large bowl, mix together 2 C. of the all-purpose flour, bread flour, corn oil and salt.
3. Add the yeast mixture and stir to combine.
4. Transfer the dough onto a smooth surface and knead well while using about 1/2 C. of the all-purpose flour.
5. Transfer the dough into a greased bowl and keep aside e in a warm place for about 2 hours.

BUFFALO GROVE
Inspired Salad Dressing

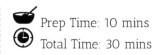

Prep Time: 10 mins
Total Time: 30 mins

Servings per Recipe: 6
Calories	662 kcal
Fat	72.3 g
Carbohydrates	4.4g
Protein	0.8 g
Cholesterol	0 mg
Sodium	334 mg

Ingredients

1 tbsp chopped fresh parsley
1 tbsp chopped green onion tops
1 tsp celery salt
1 tsp chopped fresh oregano
1 tsp chopped fresh basil
1 tbsp crushed black peppercorns
1 tbsp paprika

2 large garlic cloves, minced
2 C. olive oil
3 tbsp Burgundy wine
1/2 C. wine vinegar
1 (8 oz.) can stewed tomatoes, crushed

Directions

1. In a bowl, add the parsley, green onions, celery salt, oregano, basil, black pepper, paprika and garlic cloves and crush till a paste is formed.
2. Add the olive oil, Burgundy wine, white wine vinegar and stewed tomatoes and with an electric mixer, beat for about 5 minutes.
3. Refrigerate till serving.
4. Stir well before serving.

Illinois
Potato Burritos

Prep Time: 10 mins
Total Time: 40 mins

Servings per Recipe: 6

Calories	873 kcal
Fat	49.7 g
Carbohydrates	66.4g
Protein	40.2 g
Cholesterol	492 mg
Sodium	1291 mg

Ingredients

4 potatoes, shredded
1 small onion, finely chopped
1 clove garlic, minced
1 (8 oz.) container frozen Hatch, New Mexico green Chile peppers
1/2 C. chicken broth
12 strips turkey bacon
1/3 C. vegetable oil

1 tbsp onion powder
salt and pepper to taste
6 (10 inch) flour tortillas
butter flavored cooking spray
12 extra large eggs, beaten
2 C. shredded Cheddar cheese

Directions

1. In a large bowl of the water, place the shredded potatoes and keep aside, covered.
2. In a pan, add the onion, garlic, green chilis and chicken broth on high heat and bring to a boil.
3. Reduce the heat to low and simmer till the sauce becomes thick.
4. Remove from the heat.
5. Meanwhile, place the strips of bacon onto a paper towels lined microwave safe plate and microwave on High for about 1 minute.
6. Drain the potatoes completely.
7. In a large skillet. Heat the vegetable oil on medium-high heat.
8. Place the potatoes in the skillet and spoon the hot oil over the potatoes; evenly.
9. Sprinkle with the onion powder, salt and pepper and fry for about 15 minutes, flipping occasionally.
10. Place the tortillas between 2 damp paper towels and microwave on High for about 30 seconds.
11. Grease another skillet with the butter flavored cooking spray and heat on medium heat.

12. Cook the eggs till completely set, beating continuously.
13. Remove from the heat.
14. Arrange a tortilla onto a smooth surface.
15. Place some potatoes, scrambled egg and a bacon strip over the lower third of the tortilla, leaving about 1-inch of space from the bottom, and about 1-1/2-inch on the left and right clear for folding the burrito.
16. Top with a little of the green Chile sauce and sprinkle with the Cheddar cheese.
17. Fold the left and right edges into the middle about 1-1/2-2-inch.
18. Take the bottom edge closest to you with the filling and pick it up, pulling over, while keeping the sides in place until that edge now touches the tortilla about 7/8 of the way up to the top edge.
19. Tuck the bottom flap and seal the filling.
20. Roll the burrito up to the top edge, forming a tight cylinder.
21. Repeat with the remaining tortillas and filling ingredients.

Italian
Beef Lunch Box (Quick Roast)

🥣 Prep Time: 10 mins
🕐 Total Time: 6 hrs 10 mins

Servings per Recipe: 6
Calories	557 kcal
Fat	28.8 g
Carbohydrates	38.4g
Protein	31.9 g
Cholesterol	103 mg
Sodium	4233 mg

Ingredients

3 lbs beef chuck roast
3 (1 oz.) packages dry Italian salad dressing mix
1 C. water

1 (16 oz.) jar pepperoncini peppers
8 hamburger buns, split

Directions

1. Add your beef to the crock of a slow cooker then combine in your dressing mix. Add the water and stir.
2. Place a lid on the slow cooker and let the beef cook for 8 hours.
3. When 60 mins of cooking time remains, grab two carving forks and break the beef into pieces.
4. If you would like a more tender beef it is okay to continue cooking the meat.
5. Once the meat has been broken into pieces pour in your peppers with their associated juices.
6. Stir everything and let the meat cook for the final 60 mins.
7. Place some beef and sauce liberally on your bread with some additional pepper and salt.
8. Enjoy.

CHICAGO MERCANTILE
Inspired Cocktail

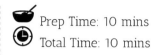

Prep Time: 10 mins
Total Time: 10 mins

Servings per Recipe: 1
Calories	284 kcal
Fat	0.1 g
Carbohydrates	30.1g
Protein	0.3 g
Cholesterol	0 mg
Sodium	14 mg

Ingredients

1 1/2 C. ice cubes
2 fluid oz. grape juice
1 fluid oz. lime juice
3/4 fluid oz. bitter orange aperitif
3/4 fluid oz. simple syrup

1/2 fluid oz. lemon juice
1/2 fluid oz. grapefruit juice
1 lemon twist for garnish

Directions

1. In a cocktail shaker, place the ice and top with the grape juice, lime juice, bitter orange aperitif, simple syrup, lemon juice and grapefruit juice.
2. Shake a few times to combine.
3. Transfer into a tall glass and serve immediately with a garnishing of the lemon twist.

Sloppy Joes
Windy City Style

Prep Time: 20 mins
Total Time: 1 hr 20 mins

Servings per Recipe: 8
Calories	367.2
Fat	17.7g
Cholesterol	77.1mg
Sodium	1489.1mg
Carbohydrates	29.9g
Protein	23.5g

Ingredients

2 lbs ground beef
3 large onions, diced
2 large green peppers, diced
1/2 C. barbecue sauce
2 tbsp Worcestershire sauce
1 1/2 tsp mustard

1 tbsp sugar
3 tbsp vinegar
1 1/2 tsp salt
20 oz. catsup (rinse bottle with water)

Directions

1. Heat a Dutch oven on medium-high heat and cook the beef till browned completely.
2. Drain the excess grease from the skillet.
3. Add the remaining all ingredients. And stir to combine.
4. Reduce the heat and simmer for about 1 1/2-2 hours.

CHICAGO CORN
Casserole

Prep Time: 15 mins
Total Time: 1 hr 15 mins

Servings per Recipe: 6
Calories	673.6
Fat	46.8 g
Cholesterol	195.0mg
Sodium	891.0mg
Carbohydrates	58.5g
Protein	10.7g

Ingredients

1 (14 3/4 oz.) cans creamed corn
1 (15 1/4 oz.) cans whole corn, drained
1 C. melted butter
3 eggs
1 C. sour cream

1 tbsp sugar
1 (8 1/2 oz.) boxes Jiffy corn muffin mix

Directions

1. Set your oven to 350 degrees F before doing anything else and grease a baking dish.
2. In a bowl, add all the ingredients and mix till well combined.
3. Transfer the mixture into the prepared baking dish evenly.
4. Cook in the oven for about 60 minutes.

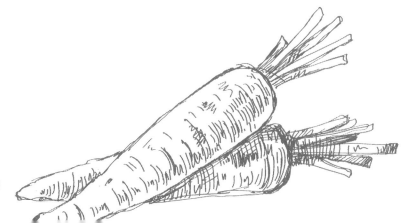

Chicago Monday
Minestrone

🍲 Prep Time: 20 mins
🕐 Total Time: 2 hrs 20 mins

Servings per Recipe: 8
Calories	301.3
Fat	14.3g
Cholesterol	11.4mg
Sodium	625.5mg
Carbohydrates	35.9g
Protein	10.4g

Ingredients

1/4 lb fresh green beans
2 medium zucchini
1 large potato
1/2 lb cabbage
1/3 C. olive oil
3 tbsp butter
2 medium onions, chopped
3 medium carrots, coarsely chopped
3 celery ribs, coarsely chopped
2 garlic cloves, minced
1 (28 oz.) cans Italian plum tomatoes, undrained
3 1/2 C. beef broth
1 1/2 C. water
1/2 tsp salt
1/2 tsp dried basil leaves, crushed
1/4 tsp dried rosemary leaves, crushed
1/4 tsp fresh black pepper
1 bay leaf
1 (16 oz.) cans cannellini beans, rinsed and drained
freshly grated Parmesan cheese

Directions

1. Trim the fresh green beans and cut into 1-inch pieces. Trim the zucchini and cut into 1/2-inch cubes. Peel the potato and cut into 3/4-inch cubes. Shred the cabbage roughly.

2. In 6 quart Dutch oven, heat the oil and butter on medium heat and cook the onions for about 6-8 minutes. Stir in the carrots and potato and cook for about 5 minutes. Stir in the celery and green beans and cook for about 5 minutes. Stir in zucchini and cook for about 3 minutes.

3. Stir in the cabbage and garlic and cook for about 1 minute. Drain the tomatoes, reserving the juice and then chop roughly.

4. Stir in the broth, water, tomatoes, reserved juice, salt, basil, rosemary, black pepper and bay leaf and bring to a boil on high heat.

5. Reduce the heat to low and simmer, covered for about 1 1/2 hours, stirring occasionally. Stir in the beans and reduce the heat to medium-low. Simmer, uncovered for about 30-40 minutes, stirring occasionally.

6. Discard the bay leaf and serve with the topping of the cheese.

5-INGREDIENT
Chicago Penne Pesto

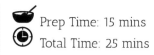

Prep Time: 15 mins
Total Time: 25 mins

Servings per Recipe: 4
Calories	856.8
Fat	14.7g
Cholesterol	91.0mg
Sodium	453.2mg
Carbohydrates	142.3g
Protein	56.5g

Ingredients

10 oz. basil pesto
1 lb penne pasta
1 lb broccoli, cut into small florets
2 (6 oz.) Tyson grilled chicken breast
strips

3 oz. shredded parmesan cheese

Directions

1. Cut the fresh broccoli buds into small florets, leaving as short a stem as possible.
2. In a large pan of lightly salted boiling water, cook the pasta for about 4-5 minutes.
3. In the last 3 minutes of the cooking, add the broccoli florets and boil for about 3 minutes.
4. Add the chicken breast strips and cook for about 1 minute.
5. Drain the pasta, mixture and transfer into a serving platter and top with the pesto.
6. Serve with a sprinkling of the shredded Parmesan cheese..

Chicago
Hot Dog Salad

Prep Time: 1 min
Total Time: 2 mins

Servings per Recipe: 8
Calories   53.0
Fat   0.9g
Cholesterol   11.1mg
Sodium   215.4mg
Carbohydrates   1.3g
Protein   9.2g

Ingredients

1/4 C. tomatoes (diced)
1/4 C. chopped dill pickle
2 tbsp chopped onions
1 tsp pickle relish
celery salt
1 celery rib, chopped

1 tbsp mayonnaise
1 tbsp mustard
2 (5 oz.) cans light chunk tuna in water

Directions

1. In a bowl, add all the ingredients and toss to coat well

CHICAGO
Mac and Cheese

Prep Time: 10 mins
Total Time: 40 mins

Servings per Recipe: 6
Calories   496.9
Fat   7.6g
Cholesterol   40.1mg
Sodium   1292.4mg
Carbohydrates   74.1g
Protein   32.0g

Ingredients

1 (14 1/2 oz.) boxes Kraft macaroni and cheese
1 (15 oz.) cans peas
1 (10 3/4 oz.) cans cream of celery soup

12 oz. tuna in water
1 C. plain breadcrumbs

Directions

1. Set your oven to 350 degrees F before doing anything else.
2. In a large pan of lightly salted boiling water, cook the macaroni till done.
3. Drain well and return to the pan.
4. Add the cheese packets according to package's directions.
5. Stir in the drained tuna, cream of celery soup and can of drained peas.
6. Transfer the mixture in a casserole dish and sprinkle with the bread crumbs evenly.
7. Cook in the oven for about 30 minutes.

Downtown Chicago
Egg Salad

🥣 Prep Time: 15 mins
🕐 Total Time: 20 mins

Servings per Recipe: 3
Calories   307.2
Fat   23.0g
Cholesterol   433.1mg
Sodium   419.3mg
Carbohydrates   11.9g
Protein   13.2g

Ingredients

6 large eggs, hard-cooked, coarsely chopped
1/4 C. diced red pepper
1/4 C. diced green pepper
1/2 C. mayonnaise
1 tbsp fresh lemon juice

2 tsp fresh snipped chives
2 tsp chopped fresh dill
1 tsp cider vinegar
salt and pepper

Directions

1. In a large bowl, mix together the eggs and peppers.
2. In another small, bowl, add the mayo, lemon juice, chives, dill and vinegar and mix till well combined.
3. Place the mayo mixture, salt and pepper in the bowl of the egg mixture and gently, stir to combine.
4. Serve immediately.

HOT TO MAKE
Chicago Pizza Dough

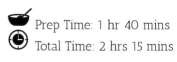 Prep Time: 1 hr 40 mins

Total Time: 2 hrs 15 mins

Servings per Recipe: 12
Calories	193.4
Fat	5.1g
Cholesterol	0.0mg
Sodium	148.6mg
Carbohydrates	32.0g
Protein	4.4g

Ingredients

1 C. warm water
2 1/4 tsp active dry yeast
3 1/2 C. all-purpose flour
1/2 C. coarse cornmeal

1 tsp kosher salt
1/4 C. canola oil

Directions

1. For Simple Method:
2. In a large bowl, dissolve the yeast in the water.
3. Add 1 C. of the flour, cornmeal, salt, and oil and mix till well combined.
4. Slowly, add the remaining flour, 1/2 C. at a time and mix till a soft dough is formed.
5. With floured hands, knead the dough for about 5-10 minutes.
6. With a plastic wrap, cover the bowl and keep aside in a warm place for about 45-60 minutes.
7. With your hands, punch and knead the dough slightly.
8. For the Bread Machine:
9. In the bread machine, place all the ingredients in the order according to manufacturer's instructions.
10. Select a 1.5-lb.-2-lb. dough cycle and press the start button.
11. Transfer the dough into a greased 15-inch deep dish pan and keep aside for about 20 minutes.
12. Set your oven to 450 degrees F.
13. Cook in the oven for about 10 minutes.
14. Remove from the oven and top the crust with your desired sauce, cheese and toppings.
15. Cook in the oven for about 15-20 minutes.
16. Now, cook under the broiler for about 5 minutes.

Rogers Park
Inspired Risotto

🥣 Prep Time: 30 mins
🕐 Total Time: 1 hr 10 mins

Servings per Recipe: 6

Calories	276.2
Fat	7.6g
Cholesterol	7.3mg
Sodium	354.1mg
Carbohydrates	41.8g
Protein	10.4g

Ingredients

3 C. vegetable broth
2 C. sliced fresh mushrooms (shitake)
1/2 C. chopped onion
2 garlic cloves, minced
2 tbsp olive oil
1 C. arborio rice
1 C. finely chopped zucchini

1 C. finely chopped carrot
1 (15 oz.) cans white kidney beans, rinsed and rained
1/2 C. grated Parmesan cheese

Directions

1. In a medium pan, add the broth and bring to a boil.
2. Reduce the heat and simmer till using.
3. Meanwhile in a large pan, heat the oil on medium heat and cook the mushrooms, onion and garlic for about 5 minutes.
4. Stir in the uncooked rice and cook for about 5 minutes.
5. Slowly, add 1 C. of the broth, stirring continuously and cook till all the liquid is absorbed.
6. Add another 1/2 C. of the broth, zucchini and carrots and cook till all the liquid is absorbed, stirring continuously.
7. Add another 1 C. of the broth, 1/2 C. at a time and cook for about 20 minutes, stirring continuously.
8. Stir in the remaining 1/2 C. broth and cook till the rice is slightly creamy and just tender, stirring continuously.
9. Stir in the white kidney beans and Parmesan cheese and cook till heated completely.

COOK COUNTY
Vegetable Mash

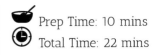

Prep Time: 10 mins
Total Time: 22 mins

Servings per Recipe: 10
Calories	301.2
Fat	17.4g
Cholesterol	49.3mg
Sodium	654.1mg
Carbohydrates	33.7g
Protein	4.9g

Ingredients

8 C. chopped red potatoes
4 C. chopped parsnips
1 rutabaga, peeled and chopped
1 onion, chopped
2 tsp salt, divided

1 (8 oz.) packages cream cheese, softened
1/2 C. butter

Directions

1. In a large Dutch oven, add the potato, parsnip, rutabaga, onion, 1 tsp of the salt and enough water to cover on high heat and bring to a boil.
2. Reduce the heat to medium-low and simmer for about 10-12 minutes.
3. Drain well and stir in the remaining salt, cream cheese and butter till the potatoes are mashed roughly.

Authentic
Chicago Style Shrimp

🥣 Prep Time: 1 hr
🕐 Total Time: 1 hr 30 mins

Servings per Recipe: 6
Calories   410.9
Fat   18.9g
Cholesterol   271.0mg
Sodium   468.4mg
Carbohydrates   16.1g
Protein   33.5g

Ingredients

2 lbs medium shrimp
1/2 C. butter, melted
1/4 C. dry sherry
2 garlic cloves, minced
2 tbsp finely chopped fresh parsley
1 tbsp finely chopped fresh chives

ground nutmeg (just a pinch)
salt, to taste
cayenne pepper, to taste
1 C. dry breadcrumbs

Directions

1. Set your oven to 350 degrees F before doing anything else and grease a 1 1/2 quart casserole dish with the melted butter.
2. In a large pan, add the shrimp and enough water to cover and gently, bring to a boil.
3. Drain into a colander and keep aside to cool slightly.
4. After cooling, peel and devein the shrimp.
5. In a bowl, add the butter, sherry, garlic, parsley, chives, nutmeg, salt and cayenne pepper and mix till well combined.
6. Add the bread crumbs and toss to coat well.
7. In the bottom of the prepared casserole dish, place half of the shrimp evenly and top with the half of the crumb mixture over the shrimp.
8. Repeat the layers once.
9. Cook in the oven for about 30 minutes.

HOW TO MAKE
Chicago Style Pizza Sauce

Prep Time: 2 mins
Total Time: 2 mins

Servings per Recipe: 10
Calories	190.0
Fat	1.0g
Cholesterol	0.0mg
Sodium	128.5mg
Carbohydrates	45.0g
Protein	7.9g

Ingredients

1 (32 oz.) cans tomato puree
1 tsp oregano
1 tsp basil
1 tsp thyme
1 tsp marjoram
1 tsp garlic powder

1 tsp pepper
Salt, to taste
1 tsp sugar

Directions

1. In a large bowl, add all the ingredients and beat till well combined.
2. Keep aside bout 2-3 hours before serving.

Chicago
Haddock Chowder

🥣 Prep Time: 20 mins
🕐 Total Time: 1 hr 20 mins

Servings per Recipe: 6

Calories	463.3
Fat	26.7g
Cholesterol	183.1mg
Sodium	1370.2mg
Carbohydrates	12.6g
Protein	42.0g

Ingredients

2 lbs haddock fillets, cut into 2 inch chunks
2 C. peeled and diced new potatoes
8 tbsp butter
1/4 C. chopped celery leaves
3 bay leaves
4 whole cloves
2 1/2 tsp salt
1/4 tsp white pepper

1 clove garlic, minced
1 C. dry vermouth, optional
2 C. boiling fish stock
2 C. half-and-half
1 1/2 tsp chopped fresh dill (to garnish)

Directions

1. Set your oven to 350 degrees F before doing anything else.
2. In a cheesecloth bag, add the celery leaves, bay leaves, and cloves tie with a kitchen string.
3. In a large casserole, mix together the fish, potatoes, butter, salt, pepper and garlic and vermouth.
4. Add the spice bag and over the casserole dish.
5. Cook in the oven for about 50-60 minutes.
6. Remove from the oven and discard the spice bag.
7. Place the boiling fish stock over the fish mixture evenly.
8. In a small pan heat the half-and-half.
9. Add the half-and-half into the chowder and stir to combine.
10. Serve immediately with a sprinkling of the dill.

CHICAGO
Chicken Cutlet

Prep Time: 20 mins
Total Time: 30 mins

Servings per Recipe: 4
Calories   439.8
Fat   28.3g
Cholesterol   73.1mg
Sodium   1074.6mg
Carbohydrates   33.5g
Protein   12.5g

Ingredients

8 chicken tenderloins
6 tbsp butter, softened
4 hoagie rolls, split
1/4 tsp oregano leaves
1/4 tsp fresh parsley, minced
12 slices hard salami
provolone cheese, halved lengthwise

1/2 C. pizza sauce
1/3 C. mushroom, fresh, sliced and sautéed
1/4 tbsp black olives, chopped

Directions

1. Set your oven to 425 degrees F before doing anything else.
2. Arrange the frozen tenderloins onto a baking sheet.
3. Cook in the oven for about 10 minutes, turning once in the middle way.
4. Spread the butter over the both halves of hoagie rolls and sprinkle bottom half with the oregano and parsley.
5. Place the salami over the bottom half, followed by the cheese slices, tenderloins, pizza sauce, mushrooms and olives.
6. Cover with the top half of roll.

Relish
for Hot Dogs Chicago Style

🥣 Prep Time: 40 mins
🕐 Total Time: 1 hr

Servings per Recipe: 100
Calories	55.9
Fat	0.0g
Cholesterol	0.0mg
Sodium	146.7mg
Carbohydrates	13.7g
Protein	0.5g

Ingredients

20 ripe tomatoes, peeled and cored
7 yellow onions, finely chopped
6 green bell peppers, finely chopped
6 C. celery, finely chopped
12 hot peppers, with seeds, finely chopped

5 1/2 C. sugar
3 C. vinegar
2 tbsp salt

Directions

1. In a food processor, add the tomatoes, onions, bell peppers, celery and hot peppers and pulse till chopped.
2. Transfer the mixture into large non-reactive pan.
3. Stir in the sugar, vinegar and salt and bring to a boil.
4. Immediately, reduce the heat and simmer till the mixture becomes thick, dark and glossy.
5. Transfer the mixture into 16 (8-oz.) hot sterile jars, leaving about 1/4-inch space from the top.
6. With a moist paper towel, wipe the rims of the jars to remove any food residue.
7. Top each jar with the hot sterile lids and screw on rings.

FRIED CHICKEN
with White Sauce

Prep Time: 15 mins
Total Time: 25 mins

Servings per Recipe: 4
Calories	188.3
Fat	15.0g
Cholesterol	91.9mg
Sodium	420.2mg
Carbohydrates	9.0g
Protein	4.5g

Ingredients

2 C. meat, minced
cayenne pepper, to taste
1 tbsp bell pepper, seeded and minced
1 egg, beaten with
1 tbsp water
breadcrumbs
WHITE SAUCE
4 tbsp butter

4 tbsp flour
1/2 tsp salt
1/8 tsp pepper
1 C. milk

Directions

1. For the sauce in a pan, melt the butter.
2. Stir in the flour, salt and pepper.
3. Slowly, add the milk, stirring continuously and cook for about 1 minute.
4. Stir in the meat, seasonings and bell pepper and remove from the heat.
5. Transfer the mixture onto a plate and keep aside to cool.
6. Shape the mixture like chicken legs and insert a wooden skewer in each leg.
7. Coat the chicken legs with the crumbs, then dip in the beaten egg and again, coat with the crumbs.
8. In a deep fryer, heat the oil to 380 degrees F ad fry the legs till desired doneness.
9. Transfer onto paper towels lined plate to drain.

Chicago Deep Dish
At-Home

🥣 Prep Time: 2 hrs 30 mins
🕐 Total Time: 2 hrs 55 mins

Servings per Recipe: 2
Calories	928.9
Fat	35.4g
Cholesterol	14.7mg
Sodium	2510.3mg
Carbohydrates	128.6g
Protein	23.3g

Ingredients

DOUGH
1/4 oz. active dry yeast
3/4 C. warm water (105-110 degrees F)
1 tsp sugar
1/4 C. corn oil
2 1/2 C. all-purpose flour
2 tsp salt
1 tsp olive oil

SAUCE
1 1/2 C. tomatoes, ground
1 tsp oregano
1 tsp basil
2 tbsp Romano cheese, grated

Directions

1. In a bowl, dissolve the yeast in sugar in the warm water.Add the corn oil and mix till well combined.Add the flour and salt and mix till a smooth and pliable dough is formed.
2. With a stand mixer, beat on medium speed for about 4 minutes.
3. Place the dough onto a smooth surface and with your hands, knead for about 2 minutes.
4. Grease a bowl with the olive oil. Place the dough ball in the bowl, turning once with the oil evenly. With a plastic wrap and towel, cover the bowl and keep aside for about 2 hours. Set your oven to 475 degrees F before doing anything else and arrange a rack in the middle of the oven.
5. Grease a 12-inch deep dish pizza pan generously. Place the dough into the prepared pizza pan and spread it across the bottom and up the sides.
6. For the sauce in a bowl, mix together the tomatoes, oregano, basil and Romano cheese.
7. Place the mozzarella and provolone over the dough crust evenly and top with the sauce and toppings evenly. Cook in the oven for about 20-25 minutes.
8. Remove from the oven and keep onto the wire rack to cool in the pan for about 3-4 minutes before cutting.

WINDY CITY
Chicago Hot Dogs

Prep Time: 15 mins
Total Time: 25 mins

Servings per Recipe: 4
Calories	298.9
Fat	14.6g
Cholesterol	22.5mg
Sodium	888.1mg
Carbohydrates	31.8g
Protein	10.8g

Ingredients

4 natural casing beef frankfurters
4 hot dog buns
1 small onion, diced fine
3 - 4 tsp sweet pickle relish
1 cold-pack kosher dill pickle, quartered
lengthwise
1 small tomatoes, sliced into julienne
strips

4 - 8 pickled sport bell peppers
brown mustard, with horseradish, to taste
celery seed
poppy seed
water, for simmering

Directions

1. In a pan, add water and frankfurters and simmer for about 10 minutes.
2. In a microwave safe plate, place the buns and microwave till slightly warm and soft.
3. Arrange 1 frankfurter in each bun and top with the mustard, followed by dill spear, relish, onion, tomato and 1-2 sport peppers.
4. Serve with a sprinkling of the celery and poppy seeds.

Italian Beef
Chicago Style (Long Roasted)

🥣 Prep Time: 10 mins
🕐 Total Time: 18 hrs 10 mins

Servings per Recipe: 12

Calories	1519.3
Fat	58.9g
Cholesterol	340.2mg
Sodium	2052.1mg
Carbohydrates	119.8g
Protein	121.5g

Ingredients

5 lbs rump roast
2 (10 1/4 oz.) cans beef consommé
1 (1 oz.) package Italian salad dressing mix
1 jar pepperoncini pepper
1 jar giardiniera

3 medium size green sweet peppers
1 loaf long thin French bread

Directions

1. Add the following to the crock of a slow cooker: rump roast, cans of beef consommé, salad dressing mix, pepperoncini, and giardiniera.
2. Let everything cook for 18 hours with a low level of heat.
3. Every 6 hours, turn the roasting beef.
4. When 2 hours of cooking time is left slice your sweet peppers and add them to the crock pot and let me cook until they are no longer hard.
5. Slice your French bread into 6 servings, then cut each serving down the middle to form the top and bottom portion of a sandwich.
6. Get 2 carving forks and begin to break up your rump roast.
7. After all the meat has been broken evenly, liberally layer beef on the sandwich and liberally add sauce as well. Finally add a bit of pepper and salt.
8. Enjoy.
9. NOTE: Do not discard the juices. Liberal application of the roasting juices will increase the tastiness of the sandwich.

BLACKHAWKS
Inspired Party Dip

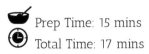

Prep Time: 15 mins

Total Time: 17 mins

Servings per Recipe: 6
Calories	208.0
Fat	14.4g
Cholesterol	51.3mg
Sodium	549.3mg
Carbohydrates	3.6g
Protein	16.0g

Ingredients

5 oz. Swanson white chicken meat packed in water, drained
10 oz. mild chunky salsa

1 1/4 oz. taco seasoning
2 C. shredded cheddar cheese

Directions

1. In a microwave safe bowl, mix together all the ingredients and microwave for about 2 minutes.

Chicago Country
Winter Soup

Prep Time: 30 mins
Total Time: 55 mins

Servings per Recipe: 6
Calories	286.2
Fat	7.2g
Cholesterol	13.1mg
Sodium	861.0mg
Carbohydrates	44.8g
Protein	12.2g

Ingredients

1 C. chopped celery
1 C. chopped onion
2 garlic cloves
1 tbsp olive oil
5 C. vegetable broth
1 C. water
1/2 C. Arborio rice
3 medium tomatoes, chopped
1 medium zucchini, chopped roughly

6 C. torn fresh spinach
1 (15 oz.) cans great northern beans, rinsed and drained
1/4 C. snipped fresh thyme
1/4 tsp cracked black pepper
1/2 C. crumbled feta cheese

Directions

1. In a Dutch oven, heat the oil and sauté the celery, onion and garlic till tender.
2. Add the broth, water and uncooked rice and bring to a boil.
3. Reduce the heat and simmer, covered for about 15 minutes.
4. Stir in the tomatoes, zucchini, torn spinach, beans, thyme and pepper and cook till heated completely.
5. Stir in the crumbled feta and serve.

CHICAGO BUTTERMILK
Pizza Bites

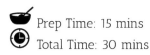

Prep Time: 15 mins
Total Time: 30 mins

Servings per Recipe: 4
Calories   208.0
Fat   14.4g
Cholesterol   51.3mg
Sodium   549.3mg
Carbohydrates   3.6g
Protein   16.0g

Ingredients

1 Pillsbury refrigerated thin pizza crust
3 1/2 oz. pepperoni
1/2 C. buttermilk ranch dressing
3 green onions, chopped

1/2 C. mozzarella cheese, shredded
1 C. Monterey jack pepper cheese, shredded

Directions

1. Set your oven to 425 degrees F before doing anything else.
2. Unroll the pizza dough onto a smooth surface.
3. Spread the ranch dressing over the dough evenly.
4. Spread pepperoni, green onions and cheese over the ranch dressing.
5. Carefully, roll the dough tightly and slice into equal sized rolls.
6. Arrange the rolls onto cookie sheet in a single layer.
7. Cook in the oven for about 15 minutes.

Chicago
Public School Pilaf

🥣 Prep Time: 20 mins
🕐 Total Time: 1 hr 5 mins

Servings per Recipe: 8
Calories   657.0
Fat   9.4g
Cholesterol   38.5mg
Sodium   47.2mg
Carbohydrates   118.1g
Protein   20.4g

Ingredients

1 lb ground beef
6 C. uncooked rice
8 oz. bell peppers in tomato sauce
2 garlic cloves (minced)
1 medium onion (chopped)
salt and pepper

3/4 tsp cinnamon
3/4 tsp allspice
3/4 tsp clove, powder
12 C. water

Directions

1. Set your oven to 350 degrees F before doing anything else.
2. Heat a large skillet and cook the beef, onion and garlic till browned completely.
3. Drain the excess grease from the skillet.
4. Stir in the tomato sauce, spices, water and rice and transfer the mixture into large baking dish.
5. Cover the baking dish and cook in the oven for about 30 - 45 minutes.

BACK-TO-SCHOOL
Cookies

Prep Time: 15 mins
Total Time: 45 mins

Servings per Recipe: 1
Calories   130.5
Fat   7.7g
Cholesterol   20.3mg
Sodium   74.3mg
Carbohydrates   14.0g
Protein   1.2g

Ingredients

1 C. softened butter
2/3 C. granulated sugar
2 C. all-purpose flour
2 tbsp all-purpose flour

2 tsp vanilla extract
1 pinch salt
4 tsp sugar

Directions

1. Set your oven to 350 degrees F before doing anything else.
2. In a bowl, add the butter and sugar and beat till fluffy.
3. Stir in the vanilla extract.
4. Slowly, add the flour and salt and mix till well combined.
5. With a small cookie scoop, roll dough into balls and arrange onto the ungreased cookie sheets in a single layer.
6. Flatten each cookie slightly with the bottom of a glass dipped in the sugar.
7. Cook in the oven for about 12-15 minutes.

Lincolnshire
Balsamic Soup

🥣 Prep Time: 15 mins
🕐 Total Time: 35 mins

Servings per Recipe: 6

Calories	281.2
Fat	11.7g
Cholesterol	51.4mg
Sodium	390.8mg
Carbohydrates	27.4g
Protein	16.6g

Ingredients

1 lb ground beef
1/2 chopped onion
3 bell peppers, any color, cored and
seeded and chopped spoon sized
14 oz. diced tomatoes
1 (8 oz.) cans tomato sauce
1 1/2 C. water
1/4 C. balsamic vinegar

1/8 tsp salt
1/8 tsp black pepper
1/4 C. brown sugar
1 C. V8 vegetable juice
1/2 C. Minute Rice

Directions

1. Heat a large skillet and cook the onion, garlic, pepper and beef till browned completely.
2. Drain the excess grease from the skillet.
3. In a pan, add the remaining ingredients except the rice and bring to a boil.
4. Stir in the rice and cover the pan.
5. Immediately, remove from the heat and keep aside for about 5 minutes.
6. Add the beef mixture into the soup pan and simmer for about 15 minutes.

CHI-TOWN
Cake

🥣 Prep Time: 10 mins
🕐 Total Time: 45 mins

Servings per Recipe: 12
Calories	323.5
Fat	15.2g
Cholesterol	52.5mg
Sodium	247.3mg
Carbohydrates	42.8g
Protein	4.6g

Ingredients

1/2 C. margarine
1 (8 oz.) packages cream cheese
1 1/4 C. sugar
2 eggs
1 tsp vanilla extract
1 3/4 C. flour
1 tsp baking powder
1/2 tsp baking soda
1/4 C. milk

Topping:
1/4 C. sugar
4 tbsp flour
4 tsp cinnamon
4 tbsp margarine

Directions

1. Set your oven to 350 degrees F before doing anything else and grease and flour a 13x9-inch baking dish.
2. In large bowl, add the margarine, cream cheese and sugar and beat till light.
3. Add the eggs and vanilla and beat till well combined.
4. In another bowl, sift together the flour, baking powder and baking soda.
5. Add the flour mixture into the egg mixture, alternately with milk and mix well.
6. For the topping in a bowl, add the sugar, flour, cinnamon and margarine and mix till a crumbly mixture is formed.
7. Place the mixture into the prepared baking dish evenly and top with the crumbly mixture.
8. Cook in the oven for about 35-40 minutes or till a toothpick inserted in the center comes out clean.

Downers Grove Steak Rolls

Prep Time: 20 mins
Total Time: 35 mins

Servings per Recipe: 8
Calories   494.8
Fat   26.4g
Cholesterol   126.7mg
Sodium   874.4mg
Carbohydrates   28.6g
Protein   34.3g

Ingredients

2 1/2 lbs round steaks, cut 1/2-inch thick
1 C. flour
1 tsp salt
1/2 tsp pepper
1 C. fresh breadcrumb
1 1/4 C. chopped onions
2 C. finely chopped butternut squash, peeled
1/4 C. chopped green pepper

1/4 C. chopped celery
1 tsp salt
1 egg, beaten
2 tbsp margarine, melted
1/4 C. margarine
1 C. water

Directions

1. Cut the meat into 8 equal sized pieces and with a meat mallet, pound into 1/4-inch thickness. In a shallow dish, mix together the flour, 1 tsp of the salt and pepper.
2. In a bowl, add the bread crumbs, onion, squash, green pepper, celery, 1 tsp of the salt, egg, and 2 tbsp of the melted margarine and mix till well combined.
3. Coat each chicken piece with the seasoned flour evenly.
4. Place the squash mixture over each chicken piece evenly.
5. Carefully, roll the chicken piece around the filling and secure with a toothpick.
6. In a 6-quart pressure cooker, melt 1/4 C. of the margarine and sear the chicken rolls till browned from all sides. Transfer the rolls into a bowl. Place 1 C. water and cooking rack in the pressure cooker. Arrange the rolls over the cooking rack.
7. Secure the lid and cook for about 35 minutes. Use the quick release method to release the pressure. Transfer the beef rolls onto the warm serving platter.
8. Transfer the pan juices into a seal pan and cook till thickened. Serve the role alongside the gravy.

ALTERNATIVE
Chicago Hot Dogs (No Bun)

Prep Time: 10 mins
Total Time: 15 mins

Servings per Recipe: 6
Calories	181.7
Fat	6.9g
Cholesterol	14.8mg
Sodium	404.0mg
Carbohydrates	24.1g
Protein	12.0g

Ingredients

6 large leaves from one head romaine lettuce
6 turkey hot dogs
1/2 C. onion, Chopped fine
1/2 C. tomatoes, diced
1/2 C. pickle, diced
1/4 C. jalapeno, seeded and diced

4 tbsp Dijon mustard
3 oz. cheddar cheese
celery seed, garnish

Directions

1. In a cast iron pan, place the hot dogs on medium heat and grill till browned from all sides with grill press.
2. Meanwhile, chop the tomatoes, jalapeños, onion and pickle and transfer into a bowl.
3. Rinse Romaine lettuce and pick out the best leaves.
4. Trim the bottom white of lettuce leaves and place onto a plate.
5. Top leaves with one hot dog, followed by tbsp of the mustard and 2 tbsp of the tomato mixture.
6. Serve with a garnishing of the celery seed and cheese.

Authentic
Italian Antipasto

🍲 Prep Time: 1 hr
🕐 Total Time: 9 hrs 30 mins

Servings per Recipe: 56
Calories	102 kcal
Fat	8.5 g
Carbohydrates	5.1g
Protein	2.1 g
Cholesterol	1 mg
Sodium	168 mg

Ingredients

4 C. diced cauliflower
4 C. pearl onions
2 C. diced red bell peppers
2 C. diced green bell peppers
2 C. diced celery
2 cucumbers - peeled, seeded and diced
2 C. carrots, diced
2 C. vegetable oil
2 C. distilled white vinegar

1 (6 oz.) can tomato paste
1 tbsp pickling spice, wrapped in cheesecloth
1 C. black olives
1 C. pitted green olives
4 C. canned mushrooms
1 1/2 (6 oz.) cans tuna, drained and flaked

Directions

1. Get a bowl, combine: cucumbers, cauliflower, celery, pearl onions, and bell peppers.
2. Submerge the mix in water and salt and let everything sit for 10 hrs.
3. Get a 2nd bowl for your carrots and let the carrots sit submerged in salt water for the same amount of time as well.
4. Now get the following boiling: pickling spice, veggie oil, tomato paste, and vinegar.
5. Once the mix is boiling add in the carrots after draining them.
6. Let the veggies cook for 12 mins.
7. Now drain the cucumber mix and add these veggies to the boiling carrots.
8. Let everything continue to cook for 12 more mins.
9. Combine in: the tuna, black olives, mushrooms, and green olives.
10. Stir the mix then shut the heat.
11. Now throw away the pickling spice and place everything in storage containers.
12. Enjoy.

CLASSICAL
Alfredo

Prep Time: 30 mins
Total Time: 1 hr

Servings per Recipe: 8
Calories	673 kcal
Fat	30.8 g
Carbohydrates	57g
Protein	43.3 g
Cholesterol	133 mg
Sodium	1386 mg

Ingredients

6 skinless, boneless chicken breast halves - cut into cubes
6 tbsps butter, divided
4 cloves garlic, minced, divided
1 tbsp Italian seasoning
1 lb fettuccini pasta
1 onion, diced
1 (8 oz.) package sliced mushrooms
1/3 C. all-purpose flour
1 tbsp salt

3/4 tsp ground white pepper
3 C. milk
1 C. half-and-half
3/4 C. grated Parmesan cheese
8 oz. shredded Colby-Monterey Jack cheese
3 roma (plum) tomatoes, diced
1/2 C. sour cream

Directions

1. Stir your chicken after coating it with Italian seasoning in 2 tbsp of butter with 2 pieces of garlic.
2. Stir fry the meat until it is fully done then place everything to the side.
3. Now boil your pasta in water and salt for 9 mins then remove all the liquids.
4. At the same time stir fry your onions in 4 tbsp of butter along with the mushrooms and 2 more pieces of garlic.
5. Continue frying the mix until the onions are see-through then combine in your pepper, salt, and flour.
6. Stir and cook the mix for 4 mins. Then gradually add in your half and half and the milk, while stirring, until everything is smooth.
7. Combine in the Monterey and parmesan and let the mix cook until the cheese has melted then add the chicken, sour cream, and tomatoes.
8. Serve your pasta topped liberally with the chicken mix and sauce.
9. Enjoy.

Easy Italian
Parmigiana

🥣 Prep Time: 30 mins
🕐 Total Time: 1 hr 30 mins

Servings per Recipe: 2
Calories   528 kcal
Fat   18.3 g
Carbohydrates   44.9 g
Protein   43.5 g
Cholesterol   184 mg
Sodium   1309 mg

Ingredients

1 egg, beaten
2 oz. dry bread crumbs
2 skinless, boneless chicken breast halves
3/4 (16 oz.) jar spaghetti sauce

2 oz. shredded mozzarella cheese
1/4 C. grated Parmesan cheese

Directions

1. Coat a cookie sheet with oil then set your oven to 350 degrees before doing anything else.
2. Get a bowl and add in your eggs.
3. Get a 2nd bowl and add in your bread crumbs.
4. Coat your chicken first with the eggs then with the bread crumbs.
5. Lay your pieces of chicken on the cookie sheet and cook them in the oven for 45 mins, until they are fully done.
6. Now add half of your pasta sauce to a casserole dish and lay in your chicken on top of the sauce.
7. Place the rest of the sauce on top of the chicken pieces. Then add a topping of parmesan and mozzarella over everything.
8. Cook the parmigiana in the oven for 25 mins.
9. Enjoy.

CLASSICAL
Spanish Beef Patties

Prep Time: 15 mins
Total Time: 45 mins

Servings per Recipe: 8

Calories	522 kcal
Fat	34.7 g
Carbohydrates	36.7g
Protein	15.9 g
Cholesterol	40 mg
Sodium	505 mg

Ingredients

3 tbsps olive oil
1 lb ground beef
1 1/2 C. diced fresh cilantro
1 onion, diced
4 cloves garlic, minced
1 green bell pepper, diced

1 (8 oz.) can tomato sauce
1 (16 oz.) package egg roll wrappers
2 quarts vegetable oil for frying

Directions

1. Stir fry your bell pepper, onions, and garlic in olive oil until tender.
2. Combine in the meat and cook the meat until it is fully done.
3. Now add the cilantro and tomato sauce.
4. Heat the contents until the cilantro is soft then place everything to the side.
5. Now add 3 tbsps of the meat mix into an egg roll wrapper and shape the wrapper into a triangle.
6. Continue doing this until all your meat has been used up.
7. Now deep fry these patties in hot veggie oil until golden on both sides. Then place the patties on some paper towels before serving.
8. Enjoy.

Pastelon
(Beef Pie from Puerto Rico)

Prep Time: 25 mins
Total Time: 1 hr 10 mins

Servings per Recipe: 2

Calories	439 kcal
Fat	14.4 g
Carbohydrates	63.8g
Protein	19.9 g
Cholesterol	221 mg
Sodium	1042 mg

Ingredients

1 onion, cut into chunks
1 green bell pepper, cut into chunks
1 bunch fresh parsley
1 bunch fresh cilantro
1 bunch recao, or cilantro
3 cloves garlic
1 tbsp water, or as needed
1 lb ground beef
1 (1.41 oz.) package sazon seasoning
ground black pepper to taste

1 pinch adobo seasoning, or to taste
olive oil
8 ripe plantains, peeled and cut on the bias
4 eggs, beaten
2 (15 oz.) cans green beans, drained
4 eggs, beaten

Directions

1. Blend the following with a blender or food processor: water, onion, garlic, bell peppers, recao, parsley, and cilantro.
2. Place the contents in a bowl with a covering of plastic and put everything in the fridge.
3. Now set your oven to 350 degrees before doing anything else.
4. Stir fry your beef until fully done then add in 2 tbsps of sofrito, adobo, sazon, and pepper.
5. Pour out any extra oils and place the beef to the side.
6. Now begin to fry your plantains for 5 mins then place half of them into a casserole dish.
7. Top the plantains with four whisked eggs and layer the beef on top.
8. Add your green beans next. Then add the rest of the plantains.
9. Finally add four more whisked eggs and also some adobo spice.
10. Cook everything in the oven for 35 mins.
11. Enjoy.

BISTEC
Encebollao (Steak and Onions)

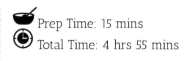

Prep Time: 15 mins

Total Time: 4 hrs 55 mins

Servings per Recipe: 6

Calories	423 kcal
Fat	32.1 g
Carbohydrates	6.3g
Protein	26.4 g
Cholesterol	81 mg
Sodium	587 mg

Ingredients

2 lbs beef sirloin steak, sliced thinly across the grain
1/2 C. olive oil
2 tbsps minced garlic
1 pinch dried oregano
1 (.18 oz.) packet sazon seasoning

2 large white onions, sliced into rings
1/4 C. distilled white vinegar
1 C. beef stock
1 tsp salt

Directions

1. Get a bowl, combine: salt, steak, beef stock, olive oil, vinegar, garlic, onions, sazon, and oregano.
2. Place a covering of plastic over the dish after stirring the beef and place everything in the fridge for 5 hrs.
3. Add all of the mix into a large frying pan and get the mix boiling.
4. Once the mix is boiling, place a lid on the pan, set the heat to low, and cook everything for 45 mins.
5. Enjoy.

Alternative
Windy City Chicken and Rice Soup

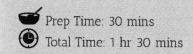 Prep Time: 30 mins

Total Time: 1 hr 30 mins

Servings per Recipe: 6
Calories	216.8
Fat	10.8g
Cholesterol	40.5mg
Sodium	476.7mg
Carbohydrates	21.7g
Protein	7.6g

Ingredients

2 quarts water
1 boneless chicken breast, skinless
1 carrot, chopped
1 stalk celery, chopped
1/2 onion, chopped
1 garlic clove, minced
1/8 C. fresh parsley, minced
1/8 C. butter

1/2 C. rice, uncooked
1 tsp salt
1 C. half-and-half cream
1/4 C. cornstarch
pepper

Directions

1. Get a Dutch oven and get your broth boiling in it. Once the broth is boiling combine in your chicken and let the chicken cook until it is fully done.
2. Once the chicken is done place it to the side to lose its heat.
3. Keep the broth in the pot.
4. Now begin to stir fry your parsley, carrots, onion, and celery in a frying pan in butter until they are soft then combine in the garlic and cook everything for 2 more mins.
5. Slice the chicken into small cubes then combine the chicken and the stir fried veggies into the broth.
6. Stir everything then add your pepper, salt, and rice.
7. Then stir everything again.
8. Get the mix gently simmering and let it cook for about 14 to 17 mins.
9. Now combine in your cornstarch and half and half.
10. Stir everything again until it is thick.
11. Enjoy.

TOSTONES
(Spanish Plantains Fried)

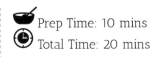
Prep Time: 10 mins
Total Time: 20 mins

Servings per Recipe: 2
Calories	136 kcal
Fat	3.3 g
Carbohydrates	28.5g
Protein	1.2 g
Cholesterol	0 mg
Sodium	14 mg

Ingredients

5 tbsps oil for frying
1 green plantain, peeled, diced into 1 inch pieces

3 C. cold water
salt to taste

Directions

1. Get your oil hot and begin to fry your plantains for 4 mins each side.
2. Place the plantains on a working surface and flatten them.
3. After all of your plantains have been flattened dip them in some water then fry the plantains again for 1 min per side.
4. Top them with salt after frying.
5. Enjoy.

Steaks
in Chicago

🥘 Prep Time: 15 mins

🕐 Total Time: 1 hr 25 mins

Servings per Recipe: 2

Calories	439 kcal
Fat	19.3 g
Carbohydrates	14.9 g
Protein	49.1 g
Cholesterol	134 mg
Sodium	142 mg

Ingredients

1 tbsp extra virgin olive oil
1 clove garlic, minced
1/2 tsp ground cinnamon
1/2 tsp white sugar
2 tbsp apricot preserves

2 (1/2 lb.) New York strip steaks, 1 inch thick
salt and pepper to taste

Directions

1. In a shallow glass dish, add the olive oil, garlic, cinnamon, sugar and apricot preserves and mix till well combined.
2. With a knife, make several shallow slashes in the steaks on both sides.
3. Sprinkle the steaks with the salt and pepper evenly.
4. Place steaks in the dish with the sauce and mix well.
5. With a plastic wrap, cover the dish and refrigerate for at least 1 hour.
6. Set your grill for high heat and lightly, grease the grill grate.
7. Cook the steaks on the grill for about 10 minutes, flipping occasionally.

Made in the USA
Monee, IL
01 October 2020